I have realized all along that the inside is more important than the body, and to the best of my ability I have stood for the things of the spirit. Yet I have felt that the physical beauty of the campus — a campus worthy of the splendid setting with which nature has endowed it, a campus worthy to be the outward frame of the University's soul, would be an education force enhancing the morale and spirit of all who come into and go forth from its halls . . . .

George Norlin, president 1919-1939

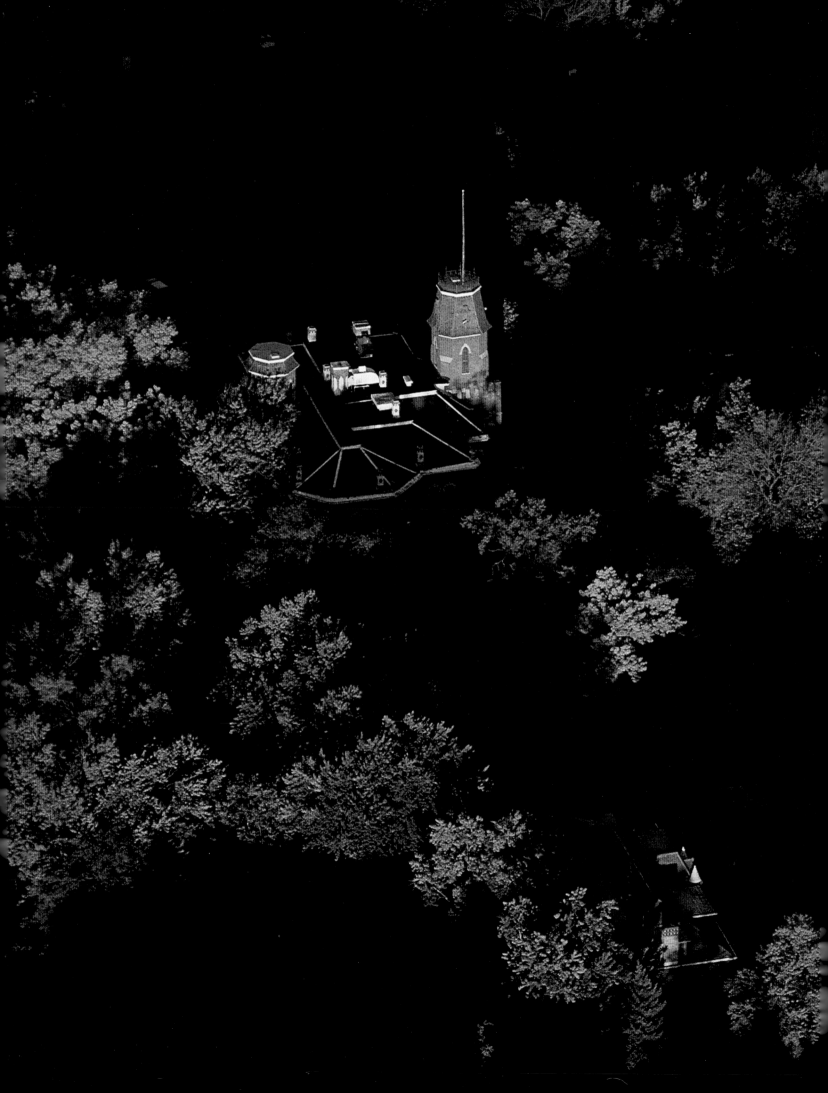

Guggenheim

University of Colorado

at Boulder

PHOTOGRAPHED BY JIM RICHARDSON

HARMONY HOUSE
PUBLISHERS - LOUISVILLE

Executive Editors: William Butler and William Strode
Library of Congress Catalog Number 89-080397
Hardcover International Standard Book Number 0-916509-54-0
Printed in Louisville, Kentucky by Fetter Printing Company
Color separations by Four Colour Imports - Louisville Kentucky
First Edition Fall 1989
Published by Harmony House Publishers, P.O. Box 90, Prospect, Kentucky 40059
(502)228-2010 / 228-4446
Copyright ©1989 Harmony House Publishers
Photographs Copyright ©1989 Jim Richardson

INTRODUCTION

By Kaye Howe
Vice Chancellor for Academic Services

We shall not cease from exploration
And the End of all our exploring
Will be to arrive where we started
And know the place for the first time.
   T.S. Eliot, "Little Gidding"

It is time which seems so important in the beginning and it is the continuous thread of our individual lives. But as time goes on, we rise above time. We recapitulate it in our memories and it becomes space, sacred space, the revered places of our recollections. None more so, for so many, than this place, our university.

It was always beautiful and always will be. We have all shared Professor Mary Rippon's response when she came here (and "here" in 1878, was one building standing alone on the high plain):

"I was almost alone in the Pullman when the train stopped. Dr. Sewall was there to meet me. The daylight had faded but a new moon cast enough light to show up the wonderful line of the snow clad mountains. The air was that of a perfect January evening, clear, dry and bracing. One of the first questions Dr. Sewall asked me was: 'How does it look to you?' With eyes turned to the silhouette at the west, and thoughts on the Alps, my one word was glorious."

In the beginning the buildings, not only of the University but the town, looked inconsequential next to these glorious mountains. And they were. Yet what was going on in those buildings was anything but inconsequential. The founding of a university in a remote, western mining town was an act of almost hubristic faith, so common to those times and this country. In 1875, Old Main rose on the plain and Horace Hale wrote:

"The University of Colorado, at Boulder, presents every appearance of being a fixed fact. This is to be a State institution, supplemental to the public schools. A beautiful building is rapidly approaching completion, erected at a cost of $35,000, by the joint appropriation of the Legislature and the citizens of Boulder. The building will be ready for occupancy in the spring, and it is the determination of its friends that the institution shall rank with the highest."

The "determination of its friends" had to withstand some difficult times. In 1893, Oscar E. Jackson, one of the first students to enter the University wrote:

"...as we look at it now, the opening of the University seemed to be an act of hardihood, not to say rashness. The population of the State barely reached one hundred

Sewall Hall

and fifty thousand. The common school system was barely organized and far from complete. But three high schools existed and an untold number of private institutions of 'higher education' were already in existence and bidding fiercely for pupils. The income of the University was less than $7,000, and in the expressive language of another, 'there was not a book for a library, not a piece of apparatus of any kind, and not a cent of money to expend for such purposes.' A naked, ill-constructed building situated in a barren waste and removed from any sidewalk by nearly a mile of mud, was all that marked the place for a future university."

In our precious early photos, Mary Rippon looks serene and assured as she gazes at us from her classroom, a phrase in an elegant hand on the blackboard, a map of Europe hanging to her right. She must, now and then, have felt very far from the elegance of Europe.

President Baker looks at us, a man who seems to know that the University is indeed a "fixed fact." He looks up from his book, his glasses off for the moment. His book comes from the wall of books behind him. Over his head hangs a copy of one of Rembrandt's self-portraits and next to it sits a classical bust. The exotic touch of a potted palm sits over his desk.

What did they see with those steady gazes? Perhaps they saw all of us coming to a place that would become more and more beautiful. Mrs. Sewall planted grass and trees and others kept up her passion to create a green and shaded place. Buildings were built and sidewalks laid and we all came, each year, to spend the best moments of our youths, that fair and difficult moment on the cusp between the adult and the child, in this garden. We've laughed and learned and talked and posed and strutted and felt highest anxiety and greatest dread and ultimate stress here. We have met our friends and our spouses, discovered our best and our worst selves.

We have come, to a degree, unformed and undiscovered and found our form and discovered the outlines of our true identities. We have left here to go off to all the wide worlds outside, some in good and some in terrible times. We carried our memories, our youths, with us. "Wherever you go," President Norlin said, "the University goes with you. Wherever you are at work, there is the University at work."

Life is a riot of exuberance here. Most of the country's issues, debates, divisions and concerns roar through here fueled by the concentration of intellect, energy and youth. War and peace, human rights, the fierce desire of oppresive groups to influence and limit the University (who will forget President Norlin's refusal to give in to the Klan when it had gained frightening political power throughout the state) all swirl about each new group of us, test each new group of us.

We come back to these buildings and trees and mountains, this air and light, because it is beautiful and because our youth is here. We were unwise here, and silly and we lacked prudence. But we had dreams, too, and visions. We were seeking, discovering, finding our place in the world.

Look into these photographs and see yourself here — always young.

Overleaf: Norlin Library

It is difficult to define a university. It is at once a place, an atmosphere and a tradition . . .

The University of Colorado is a place where the freedoms to teach and to learn have been carefully maintained. It has always had security and a modest pride of achievement. Its product through the years has been men and women of solid attainments, living lives of usefulness and contributing greatly to the betterment of their communities and to mankind generally.

President Robert L. Stearns, Statement on Academic Freedom,
Colorado Alumnus, May 1951

The beautiful grounds stretching almost to the foot of rugged peaks present a never-to-be-forgotten sight. Visitors long remember the backdrop of snow-capped peaks... the low rambling sandstone buildings with their red tile roofs... acres of green grass, shrubs, trees... and over all the puff clouds in the Colorado blue sky... almost intangible things make up pleasant memories of the campus.

Colorado Alumnus, January 1951

Sibell Wolle Fine Arts Building

Fiske Planetarium

My opinion is that schools are responsible not only for presenting organized knowledge, but also for the kind of individuals that they turn out — for the attitudes these individuals have toward society. These two functions cannot be separated; they are subtly interwoven. But more important, organized knowledge has significance only when it relates itself to goals and ideals.

Dean Jacob Van Ek, 1935

Steve Jones, Journalism

CONSERVATION · OF ·

$$P = I\omega$$

$$\underline{\omega} = \text{ANGULA}$$

$$I = \sum_i m_i r_i^2$$

BIKE WHEEL

$$= r^2 \sum_i m_i = r^2 M$$

DISK

M, SAME r.

Albert Bartlett, Physics

ANGULAR MOMENTUM

R VEL. IN RAD/SEC

OF INERTIA.)

M IS ALL AT

$$= \int_{\Lambda=0}^{\Lambda=\Lambda} \Lambda^2 dm \qquad \rho =$$

$$dm = 2\pi$$

Heritage Center

Macky Auditorium

Overleaf: Macky Auditorium Concert Hall

We have never even remotely considered a departure from the basic architecture at Boulder. Quite the contrary, we are going to do everything within our power to preserve the features of which the University, its alumni, and the state are very proud.

This architectural style (known as Italian Renaissance), adopted many years ago, has made our campus one of the most beautiful in the world, and our whole aim is to preserve its beauty.

President Quigg Newton, 1961

Norlin Library

Old Main

UMC Founatin

Farrand Hall

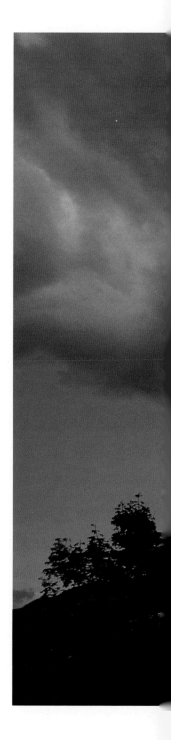

Duane Physics Building

Mary Rippon Theatre

Gilbert and Sullivan Festival

Overleaf: Charlotte Irey Dance Studios

Scenery and climate, those geographical magnets which have long drawn streams of tourists, thousands of new residents and hundreds of new businesses into Colorado, are now being supplemented by a man-made magnetism whose lines of force radiate from Colorado into all parts of the world.

This new force, which is centered in the University of Colorado, has attracted — and is attracting — sufficient numbers of top-flight scientists and scientific organizations so that the development of Boulder into one of the nation's leading centers of science is now a realistic possibility and not just a wishful dream.

Alumnus Wayne E. Johnson, in *The Denver Post*, 1961

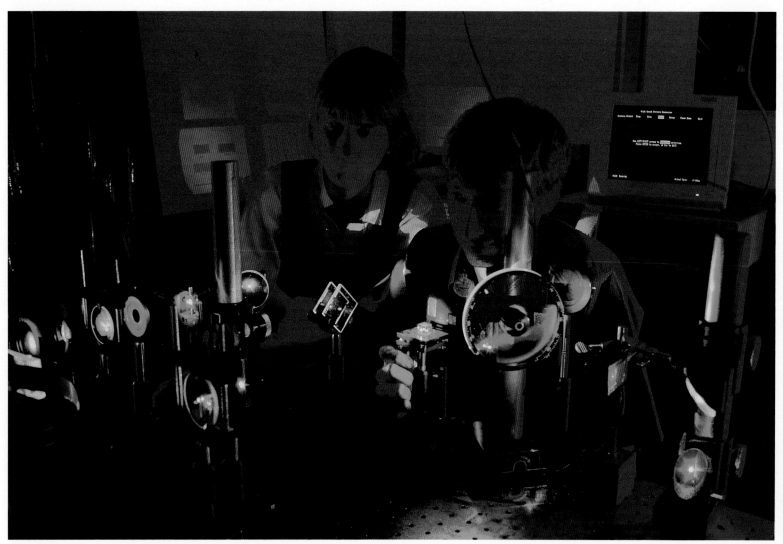

Kristina Johnson, Optoelectronic Computing Systems Center

Preceding Pages: Sibell Wolle Fine Arts Building

John Taylor, Physics

There stands my Alma Mater as I knew her in days of old, upon that very mesa, within the shadow of the same majestic mountains, somewhat cared by age . . . yet as imposing as in days of yore. But she is no longer lonely, for grouped around her on a campus of exquisite beauty, once a field of boulders and a treeless tract, are many stately halls of learning; toward the mountains on a commanding slope of the mesa, hundreds of homes for culture and refinement greet the eyes, and below, a modern bustling city . . .

Henry Drumm, Class of 1882

65

Farrand Hall

Sewall Hall

I was almost alone in the Pullman when the train stopped. Dr. Sewall was there to meet me. The daylight had faded but a new moon cast enough light to show up the wonderful line of the snowclad mountains. The air was that of a perfect January evening, clear, dry, and bracing. One of the first questions Dr. Sewall asked me was: "How does it look to you?" With eyes turned to the silhouette at the west, and thoughts on the Alps, my one word was "glorious."

Professor Mary Rippon, 1878

Heritage Center

Boulder Mall

The Hill

Downtown Boulder

The Sink

Norlin Library

Alferd Packer Day

Our task is to continue to keep our total program on a high level, one which effectively supplements the exciting work that goes on in our classrooms, our libraries and our laboratories. In doing so, we must recognize that we as a nation do not accept defeat with equanimity — even when it relates to schoolboy games. May we never lose our intense will to win, be it in our more serious pursuits or in our recreations. In this respect, there need be no cause for conflict provided that we have the insight and the discipline to give our serious pursuits precedence. This we have done, and are doing, at Colorado.

Dean Harry Carlson, *Colorado Alumnus,* March-April, 1958

Sal Aunesse, 1968-1989

Reuben Zubrow, Economics

John Rohner, Museum

Howard Higman, Political Science

David Carrasco, Religious Studies

89

The University is not the campus, not the buildings on the campus, not the students of any one time — not one of these or all of them. The University consists of all who come into and go forth from her halls, who are touched by her influence and who carry her spirit. Wherever you go, the University goes with you. Wherever you are at work there is the University at work. What the University purposes to be, what it must always strive to be, is represented on its seal, which is stamped on your diplomas — a lamp in the hands of youth. If its light shines not in you and from you, how great is its darkness! But if it shines in you, who can measure its power? With hope and faith, I welcome you into fellowship.

President George Norlin, Charge to Graduates, June, 1935

A BACKWARD GLANCE

A Selection of Vintage Photographs from the University of Colorado at Boulder Alumni Association's Heritage Center

Looking west at 15th and Pearl Street, downtown Boulder, in 1893.

Historical information from CU Heritage Center Director
Nancy Markham and Professor Albert A. Bartlett. Many
of the photos taken from the turn of the century are by
J.R. Brackett, first Dean of Liberal Arts.

Old Main, still new and relatively isolated here in 1880, was completed in April, 1876.
(Photo by Alex Martin)

Cottage #2, shown here in 1884, stood on the site of the present Economics Building. The building was torn down in the late 1920s.

The Law Lecture Room, probably in the original 1884 wing of the Medical Building, which was used by the Law School before it moved to Hale in 1893.

The math classroom of Professor Ira De Long in Old Main, in the spring of 1893.

Mary Rippon, professor of German, in her classroom (probably in Old Main), 1892.

Cottage #1, built in 1884 as a women's dormitory and dining hall. This building today houses Women's Studies.

Interior of Cottage #1 around 1893, showing the dining hall. The columns are still in place today.

President Baker in his office in the early 1900s. The office was located in what is now the Koenig Alumni Center.

The interior of the first library as it looked in 1904. The building is now the University Theatre.

Looking southeast in 1898 at the old Anatomy Building that stood in the quadrangle formed today by the Theatre, Hellems, and Chemistry. An unidentified gentleman stands with Helen Richardson, Blanche Ricketts, and Nellie Drake.

A typical student's room, 1893. This photo was taken in Woodbury Hall.

This is the old Chemistry Building in 1898. At left can be seen the fence around Gamble Field, and off in the distance is the Chautauqua Auditorium, which was completed this same year.

Colorado vs. Nebraska, 1902. Taken from the roof of Old Main, this photo shows the old Chemistry Building and the Anatomy Building with the game in play on Gamble Field. Colorado lost this game, 10-0.

The 1894 University of Colorado baseball team.

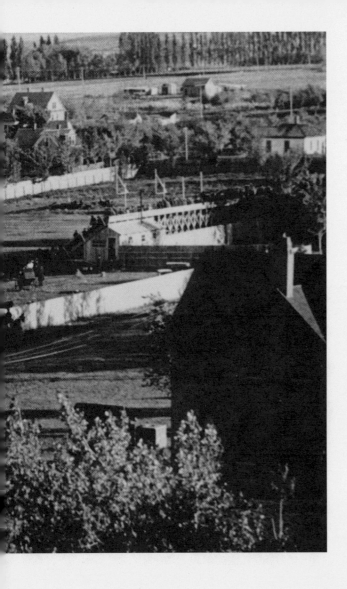

(Left) William W. "Billy" Kidd (Econ '69) and James F. "Jimmie" Heuga (A&S '73), Olympic medalists at the 1964 Winter Games in Innsbruck, Austria.

Football on Gamble Field at the turn of the century. The Anatomy Building is in the background (left) with Old Main (right).

A 1908 view of University (Varsity) Lake, Main Building and the Library.

The Library in the fall, 1906.

I remember especially Old Main, with its very tall windows and their elegant inside shutters, and the sunlight trickling through, and the student body assembled each morning for chapel, all the faculty sitting on the stage, all the students including the professional schools seated in the chapel.

The faculty took turns in conducting chapel — there was Dr. Norlin, Dr. Hellems, Dr. Taylor — all young men then, not much older than we were; and Dr. Brackett, Dr. Ayre, Prof. DeLong and the others, all stalwarts of long ago.

And yet it doesn't seem so long ago. In fifty short years we have grown into this splendid university with its lovely campus and it seems to one that with these giant strides of our Alma Mater, we ourselves are going to have to hurry to keep up.

Elizabeth Ricketts '01

Old Main chapel with elegant archway at the center stage.

Old Main, in a photo taken from the upper floor of Hale looking east, before 1910.

Woodbury Hall, 1905

The President's House (now Koenig Alumni Center) around 1910.

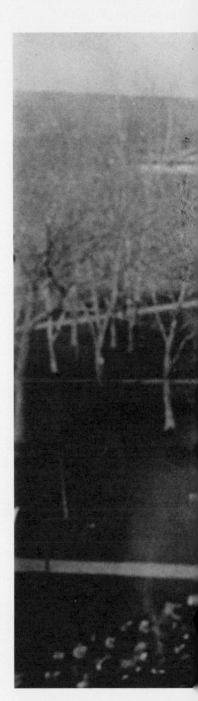

Graduation or May Day festivities on the Quadrangle, circa 1912.

Macky Auditorium from the plain by Boulder Creek.

Remember when we went to Macky Auditorium to watch a football game being played in Utah? A moving light on a large, gridironed board showed the location of the ball as the plays were telegraphed in. How the light brought the house down as it showed "Whizzer" White taking a punt, going back, and then outrunning the whole field for a touchdown!"

Wilfred Rieder '34, in a letter to *The Colorado Alumnus*, 1982

Byron White, A&S '38, Rhodes Scholar 1938-39, NFL Hall of Fame 1954, appointed to Supreme Court 1962, CU's Centennial Alumnus 1987.